Frederick E. Haynes

The Reciprocity Treaty with Canada of 1854

Frederick E. Haynes

The Reciprocity Treaty with Canada of 1854

ISBN/EAN: 9783337192686

Printed in Europe, USA, Canada, Australia, Japan

Cover: Foto ©ninafisch / pixelio.de

More available books at **www.hansebooks.com**

PUBLICATIONS

OF THE

AMERICAN ECONOMIC ASSOCIATION.

VOL. VII. No. 6. {

SIX NUMBERS A YEAR.
PRICE $4.00 A YEAR.

THE

Reciprocity Treaty with Canada

of 1854.

BY

FREDERICK E. HAYNES, PH. D.

AMERICAN ECONOMIC ASSOCIATION,

November, 1892.

BALTIMORE:
FROM THE PRESS OF GUGGENHEIMER, WEIL & CO.
1892.

TABLE OF CONTENTS.

The Reciprocity Treaty with Canada of 1854.

The treaty concluded between the United States and Great Britain on June 5. 1854, was designed to regulate the commercial relations between the United States and the British possessions in North America. It was negotiated at Washington by William L. Marcy, Secretary of State of the United States, and by the Earl of Elgin and Kincardine, Governor-General of the North American provinces, acting for their respective governments.

The treaty consisted of seven articles, of which the first two related to the fisheries, the third to reciprocal trade, the fourth to the navigation of the St. Lawrence, the fifth to the duration and abrogation of the treaty, the sixth to the extension of the provisions of the treaty to Newfoundland, if that colony indicated a desire for such extension, and the last article to the ratification of the treaty.

The third and fourth articles, to the discussion of which I intend to devote this paper, are as follows:

ART. III. It is agreed that the articles enumerated in the schedule hereunto annexed, being the growth and produce of the aforesaid British colonies, or of the United States, shall be admitted into each country respectively free of duty.

SCHEDULE.

Grain, flour and breadstuffs of all kinds.
Animals of all kinds.
Fresh, smoked and salted meats.
Cotton-wool, seeds and vegetables.

Undried fruits, dried fruits.

Fish of all kinds.

Products of fish and all other creatures living in the water.

Poultry, eggs.

Hides, furs, skins, or tails, undressed.

Stone or marble, in its crude or unwrought state.

Slate.

Butter, cheese and tallow.

Lard, horns, manures.

Ores of metals of all kinds.

Coal.

Pitch, tar, turpentine, ashes.

Timber and lumber of all kinds, round, hewed and sawed, unmanufactured in whole or in part.

Firewood.

Plants, shrubs and trees.

Pelts, wool.

Fish-oil.

Rice, broom-corn and bark.

Gypsum, ground or unground.

Hewn or wrought or unwrought burrs or grindstones.

Dyestuffs.

Flax, hemp and tow, unmanufactured; unmanufactured tobacco.

Rags.

ART. IV. It is agreed that the citizens and inhabitants of the United States shall have the right to navigate the river St. Lawrence and the canals of Canada, used as the means of communication between the great lakes and the Atlantic ocean, with their vessels, boats and crafts, as fully and freely as the subjects of Her Brittanic Majesty, subject only to the same tolls and other assessments as now are, or may hereafter be, exacted of Her Majesty's said subjects; it being understood, however, that the British government retains the right of suspending this privilege on giving due notice thereof to the government of the United States.

It is further agreed that if at any time the British government should exercise the said reserved right, the government of the United States shall have the right of suspending, if it thinks fit, the operation of Article III of the present treaty, in so far as the province of Canada is affected thereby, for so long as the suspension of the free navigation of the river St. Lawrence or the canals may continue.

It is further agreed that British subjects shall have the right freely to navigate Lake Michigan with their vessels, boats and crafts so long as the privilege of navigating the river St. Lawrence, secured to American citizens by the above clause of the present article shall continue; and the government of the United States further engages to urge upon the state governments to secure to the subjects of Her Brittanic Majesty the use of the several state canals on terms of equality with the inhabitants of the United States.

And it is further agreed that no export duty, or other duty, shall be levied on lumber or timber of any kind cut on that portion of the American territory in the state of Maine, watered by the river St. John and its tributaries, and floated down that river to the sea, when the same is shipped to the United States from the province of New Brunswick.[1]

HISTORY OF THE TREATY.

Previously to 1845 the trade between the United States and British provinces was burdened with a system of differential duties which discriminated against foreign importations into Canada in favor of British to such an extent as to prevent any, extensive trade.

In 1845 the British government changed its commercial policy by authorizing the Canadian legislature to regulate its own tariff. In 1847 the Canadian legislature removed the existing differential duties, and admitted American goods on the same terms as those imported from Great Britain.

This change of policy seems to have been the result of two causes; (1) of that change of policy in England which manifested itself in the abolition of the Corn laws in 1846, and in the repeal of the Navigation laws in 1849; and (2) of local causes in Canada. The Canadian rebellion of 1838-39 was the result of the long continued hostility between the English in Upper Canada and the French in Lower Canada.

[1]"Treaties and Conventions of the United States."   pp. 448-453.

The attempt of Pitt in 1791 to settle the dispute by dividing Canada into two provinces had failed. The long pent-up feeling broke out in open rebellion in both the provinces. To pacify the people the British government decided to reunite the two provinces and give to the consolidated province a responsible government in accordance with the recommendation of Lord Durham's report of 1839. This was done in 1840.

The constitutional grievances were, however, not the only ones. The people of Canada saw, with increasing discontent, the rapid strides of the United States in wealth. They longed to share in that progress, and hence the desire of annexation began to be felt. Lord Elgin, the governor-general from 1847-1854, recognized the conditions, and through his efforts the Reciprocity Treaty of 1854 was negotiated, giving to the people some of the advantages possessed by their more fortunate and richer neighbors.

In March, 1849, Lord Elgin called Lord Grey's attention to the subject:

"There has been," he writes, "a vast deal of talk about 'annexation,' as is unfortunately always the case here when there is anything to agitate the public mind. . . . A great deal of this talk is, however, bravado, and a great deal the mere product of thoughtlessness. Undoubtedly it is in some quarters the utterance of very serious conviction; and if England will not make the sacrifices which are absolutely necessary to put the colonists here in as good a position commercially as the citizens of the States—in order to which *free navigation* and *reciprocal trade with the states are indispensable*—if not only the organs of the league, but those of the government, and of the Peel party, are always writing as if it were an admitted fact that colonies, and more especially Canada, are a burden, to be endured only because they cannot be got rid of, the end may be nearer than we wot of."[1]

_____

"Letters and Journals of Lord Elgin." Edited by T. Walrond. London, 1872. pp. 100, 102 and 104.

Again, in November of the same year, he writes:

"But if things remain on their present footing in this respect, there is nothing before us but violent agitation, ending in convulsion or annexation. . . . And I much fear that no measure but the establishment of reciprocal trade between Canada and the States, or the imposition of a duty on the produce of the States when imported into England, will remove it."[1]

Such being the state of feeling in Canada in regard to matters of trade, the address[2] of the Parliament to the Queen, praying that the prospective changes in the laws regulating the admission of foreign grain into the British markets might be made with some reference to their needs, came as a natural consequence. This address also contained a specific request for the opening of negotiations with the United States for the admission of the products of either country into the ports of the other upon equal terms. This address, made on May 12, 1846, received a favorable answer on June 3, 1846, and thus became the first direct step in the negotiation of the reciprocity treaty.

Accordingly, in December, 1846, the British minister, Mr. Pakenham, acting under instructions, communicated with the Secretary of the Treasury, Robert J. Walker, upon the subject. The United States government proved to be favorably disposed to the proposition for freer trade with Canada, and upon consultation it was decided to proceed by means of concurrent legislation by the United States and Canada. Steps were therefore taken for the completion of this plan.

---

[1] "Letters and Journals of Lord Elgin." Edited by T. Walrond. London, 1872. pp. 100, 102 and 104.

[2] "House Executive Documents." First Session Thirty-first Congress. Vol. VIII, No. 64, p. 2. 1849-50.

In 1847 the Canadian Parliament, immediately availing itself of the power conferred upon it by the Imperial government, to regulate duties on the products both of foreign countries and of the mother country, the duties on American manufactures were lowered from 12½ to 7½ per cent., and those on British manufactures were raised from 5 to 7½, thus placing the United States on an equality with the mother country.[1]

The memorandum of the Hon. W. H. Merritt, submitted to the United States in the summer of 1849, contains a copy of an act of the Canadian Parliament "to provide for the free admission of certain articles of the growth or production of the United States of America into Canada, whenever similar articles, the growth and production of Canada, shall be admitted without duty into the said States."[2]

In 1848 a bill was drawn up by the committee on commerce of the House of Representatives, and strongly recommended by the Secretary of the Treasury. This bill passed the House without opposition in 1848, but failed to receive the attention of the Senate on account of the pressure of other business. At the next session it again failed to be acted upon by the Senate for the same reason.[3]

In January, 1850, a similar bill was reported by the committee on commerce, and recommitted "with a view to provide therein for the free navigation of the river St. Lawrence, and to assimilate the same to the bill now pending before the Senate of the like

[1] "House Executive Documents." First Session Thirty-first Congress. Vol. VIII, No. 64, pp. 3–4.

[2] Same, p. 14.

[3] "House Executive Documents." First Session Thirty-first Congress. Vol. VIII, No. 64, p. 3.

character." The committee on commerce, through
its chairman, Robert M. McLane, requested the Secretary of State to inform it upon the subject of the
navigation of the St. Lawrence. Secretary Clayton,
after communication with the British minister, informed the committee of the readiness of the British
government to concede the navigation by treaty.[1]
The introduction of this new feature seems to have
caused the first consideration of a treaty in reference
to the pending negotiations.

Finally at the next session the subject was taken
up again as a matter of legislation by the introduction in the House of a bill for reciprocity of trade
between the United States and Canada and for the
free navigation by American vessels of the canals
and waters of Canada. Late in the session the matter was debated, and an amendment suggested, which
provided for the importation of American manufactures into Canada at the same rates as those at which
British manufactures were imported.[2]

After 1851 no serious attempt was made to obtain
reciprocal trade by means of concurrent legislation.
There were probably two principal reasons for this
neglect, (1) the disturbed political condition of the
times, and (2) the situation in regard to the north-
eastern fisheries, arising from differences in interpre-
tation of the convention of 1818.

The beginning of the negotiations in regard to reciprocity had arisen from the discontent in Canada,
but the introduction of the question of the fisheries

---

[1] *Congressional Globe.* First Session Thirty-first Congress. Part
II, page 1009. 1849–50.

[2] *Congressional Globe.* Second Session Thirty-first Congress. Vol.
XXIII, p. 22, 150–51. 1850–51.

interested the maritime provinces exclusively. In this way the negotiation became extended so as to include all the British possessions in North America. It is probable, however, that without the existence of the fishery problem, the maritime provinces would have been included in any reciprocity measure, for in 1849 the British chargé d'affaires, writing to the Secretary of State, says that he has lately received an instruction directing him, with the concurrence of the lieutenant governor of New Brunswick, to negotiate for the extension of reciprocity to that province upon the same conditions for which it may be conceded to Canada.[1]

Just at the end of the session of Congress in 1853, Mr. Breckinridge moved for the suspension of the rules for the introduction of the resolution requesting the President "to arrange by treaty the questions connected with the fisheries on the coasts of British North America. the free navigation of the St. Lawrence and St. John, the export duty on American lumber in the province of New Brunswick, and reciprocal trade with the British North American colonies on the principles of liberal commercial intercourse."

Finally the English government determined to send the Earl of Elgin, then governor-general of Canada, to Washington. The party on leaving England consisted only of Lord Elgin, Mr. Francis Hincks, then prime minister of Canada, Captain Hamilton, A. D. C., and Lawrence Oliphant, private secretary of Lord Elgin; but at New York it was joined by Colonel

Bruce and one or two Canadians, whose advice and
assistance upon commercial questions were needed.[1]
Upon arriving at Washington Lord Elgin announced
the object of his visit to President Pierce and the
Secretary of State, Mr. Marcy, who told him that it
was entirely hopeless to expect that such a treaty as
he proposed could be carried through with the opposition which existed to it on the part of the Democrats, who had a majority in the Senate. They as-
sured him, however, that if he could overcome this
opposition he would find no difficulty with the executive branch of the government. With this object in
view, the conversion of the Democratic majority in
the Senate, "Lord Elgin and his staff approached the
representatives of the American nation with all the
legitimate wiles of accomplished and astute diplo-
macy. They threw themselves into the society of
Washington with the abandon and enjoyment of a
group of visitors solely intent on pleasure." "At
last, after several days of uninterrupted festivity,"
writes Oliphant, "I began to perceive what we were
driving at. To make quite sure, I said one day to
my chief, 'I find all my most intimate friends are
Democratic Senators.' 'So do I,' he replied drily."[2]

In a letter written at the time Oliphant describes
more minutely the methods used by Lord Elgin in his
personal intercourse with those whom he wished to
bring over to his side: "Lord Elgin pretends to
drink immensely, but I watched him, and I don't
believe he drank a glass between two and twelve.

[1] These gentlemen were intended to act as delegates from the different provinces to advise in regard to matters concerning them.
"Reminiscences of Sir Francis Hincks." pp. 234 and 315.

[2] "Episodes in a Life of Adventure." Lawrence Oliphant. 1887.
p. 40.

He is the most thorough diplomat possible,—never loses sight for a moment of his object, and while he is chaffing Yankees and slapping them on the back, he is systematically pursuing that object. The consequence is, he is the most popular Englishman that ever visited the United States."[1]

At last, after about ten days of social activity, Lord Elgin informed Mr. Marcy that if the government was prepared to adhere to its promises to conclude a reciprocity treaty with Canada, he could assure the President that a majority of the Senate would be found favorable to it. "Mr. Marcy," says Oliphant, "could scarcely believe his ears, and was so much taken aback that I somewhat doubted the desire to make the treaty, which he so strongly expressed on the occasion of Lord Elgin's first interview with him, when he also pronounced it hopeless."[2] The next three days were occupied with the arrangement of the details of the treaty, which had to be hurried through, as Lord Elgin was due at the seat of his government.[3]

"We are tremendously triumphant; we have signel a stunning treaty. When I say we, it was in the dead of night, in the last five minutes of the fifth of June, and the first five minutes of the sixth day of the month aforesaid, that in a spacious chamber, by the brilliant light of six wax candles and an Argand, four individuals might have been observed seated, their faces expressive of deep and earnest thought not unmixed with cunning. Their feelings, however, to the acute observer, manifested themselves in different ways; and

[1] "Life of Lawrence Oliphant," by Mrs. M. O. W. Oliphant. 1891. p. 120.

[2] "Episodes in a Life of Adventure." pp. 43–44.

[3] The principal cause of the failure of former negotiations arose from the refusal of the British government to treat, unless the coal of New Brunswick and Nova Scotia were included in the free list. "Reminiscences of His Public Life," by Sir Francis Hincks. p. 233. Montreal. 1884.

this was but natural, as two were young and two aged,—one, indeed, far gone in years, the other prematurely so. He it is whose measured tones alone break the solemn silence of midnight, except when one of the younger auditors, who are intently poring over voluminous MSS., interrupts him to interpolate 'and' or scratch out 'the.' They are, in fact, checking him, and the aged man listens while he picks his teeth with a pair of scissors. or clears out the wick of the candles with their points and wipes them on his hair. He may occasionally be observed to wink, either from conscious 'cuteness or unconscious drowsiness. Attached to these three MSS. by red ribbons are the heavy seals. Presently the clock strikes twelve, and there is a doubt whether to date it to-day or yesterday. For a moment there is a solemn silence, and he who was reading takes the pen, which has previously been impressively dipped in the ink by the most intelligent of the young men, who appears to be his secretary, and who keeps his eyes wearily upon the other young man, who is the opposition secretary, and interesting as a specimen of a Yankee in that capacity. There is something strongly mysterious in the scratching of that midnight pen, for it is scratching away the destinies of nations; and then it is placed in the hands of the venerable file, whose hand does not shake, though he is very old, and knows he will be bullied to death by half the members of Congress. The hand that has used a revolver upon previous occasions does not waver with a pen, though the lines he traces may be an involver of a revolver again. He is now the Secretary of State; before that, a general in the army; before that, governor of a state; before that Secretary of War; before that, minister to Mexico; before that, a member of the House of Representatives; before that an adventurer; before that a cabinet-maker. So why should the old man fear? Has he not survived the changes and chances of more different sorts of lives than any other man? and is he afraid of being done by an English lord? So he gives us his blessing, and we leave the old man and his secretary with our treaty in our pockets."[1]

In this rather grandiloquent style Oliphant described the signing of the treaty in a letter written to his mother upon June 7, 1854.

Doubts have been expressed as to the means employed in the negotiation of the treaty. Enemies of Lord Elgin at home and in the provinces said that it

---

[1] "Memoir of the Life of Lawrence Oliphant, and Alice Oliphant, his Wife," by Margaret O. W. Oliphant. Vol. I, pp. 130–132.

was bought with British gold. American opponents of the treaty declared that it was "floated through on champagne." While there is no reason to believe that open bribery was used, there does appear to be ample evidence that the second charge was well founded, and Lord Elgin's secretary does not hesitate to admit its substantial truth, for he says in his account of the negotiations that "without altogether admitting this, there can be no doubt that in the hands of a skillful diplomatist that liquor is not without its value."[1]

Although the means used in the negotiation of the treaty were not such as to reflect credit upon those engaged in them, the preceding attempts to obtain reciprocal trade privileges show that it had a substantial movement behind it and was not merely "floated through on champagne." An act to carry the treaty into effect was passed by Congress and approved by the President, August 5, 1854. This act (Thirty-third Congress, First Session, Chapter 259, 1854), provided that—

" Whenever the President of the United States shall receive satisfactory evidence that the Imperial Parliament of Great Britain and the Provincial Parliaments of Canada, New Brunswick, Nova Scotia and Prince Edward's Island have passed laws on their part to give full effect to the provisions of the treaty between the United States and Great Britain, ... he is hereby authorized to issue his proclamation declaring that he has such evidence, and thereupon, from the date of such proclamation," the provisions of the treaty should take effect.[2]

The President issued his proclamation March 16, 1855.[3]

[1] "Life of Oliphant," p. 109.   "Episodes in a Life of Adventure," p. 38.

[2] "Statutes at Large," Vol. X, pp. 587-88, 1851-55.

[3] "Statutes at Large," Vol. 10, p. 1179. Acts to carry into effect the treaty were passed by Canada, September 23, 1854; Prince Edward

For the first few years the treaty seems to have been popular. The condition of the country remained prosperous. In 1857, however, came the great crisis of that year, and before the country had fairly recovered from the effects of that disturbance, the slavery question had reached such a stage that war alone could settle it. The "irrepressible conflict" came and the reciprocity treaty was doomed. As we shall see later, the treaty was far from satisfactory, even to its friends, looking at it from a purely economic point of view. But it would never have been abrogated on account of its defects, for those could have been remedied by negotiation. It fell a victim "to the anger which the behavior of a party in England had excited in America."[1] Moreover, there were the inevitable commercial disturbances of a time of war.

One slight attempt was made in 1858 to extend reciprocity; but it failed. The first proposition, made May 18, proposed to place certain products upon a footing with the articles exempted from duty under the reciprocity treaty of 1854. The second proposition was in the form of a joint resolution authorizing the President, "whenever he shall receive satisfactory information that hay and hops, being the products of the United Sates, and exported thence to any of the British North American provinces, are admitted

Island. October 7, 1854; New Brunswick, November 3, 1854; Nova Scotia, December 13, 1854; and Newfoundland, July 7, 1855. "British and Foreign State Papers," 1854-55, Vol. XLV, pp. 878-884. The treaty passed the Colonial legislatures with a total of only 21 dissentient votes. "Episodes in a Life of Adventure," Oliphant, pp. 52-53. The principal opposition came from Nova Scotia, and was due to the fisheries clauses. "Hinck's Reminiscences," pp. 233-36.

[1] "Canada and the Canadian Question." Goldwin Smith, p. 141.

free of duty, to issue his proclamation declaring hay and hops, the products of those provinces, shall be admitted free of duty."[1]

In March, 1860, the House passed a resolution requesting the President to give it all the information in his possession relative to the working of the treaty. Particular information was requested as to "Whether the provincial government of Canada has not, through its legislature, violated the spirit of said treaty; what has been the practical effect of the third clause upon the interests of the respective countries; what measures, if any, have been taken to procure correct information touching the practical operation and effect of the third article upon the interests of the American citizens, and whether, in his opinion, the third article could not, with advantage to Amercan interests, be either amended or rescinded.[2]

From this time on until the final abrogation of the treaty, it remained a frequent subject of controversy between the friends and opponents of the reciprocity policy. Elaborate reports were made from time to time by the committee on commerce of the House. Of these reports the most exhaustive was that prepared by Elijah Ward, of New York, for the committee on commerce, and presented to the House on February 5, 1862.[3] This report states in a clear and thorough manner the position of the friends of the treaty. Mr. Ward, while criticising many of the features of the treaty, and especially referring to the

---

[1] *Congressional Globe*, First Session, Thirty-fifth Congress, pp. 2212 and 3016. Part III.

[2] *Congressional Globe*, First Session, Thirty-sixth Congress, p. 1357. Part II.

[3] "House Reports of Committee," Second Session, Thirty-seventh Congress, 1861-2. Vol. III, No. 22.

hostile policy of Canada in discriminating against American vessels using its canals under the provision for free navigation, believed in the general soundness of the policy of reciprocity, and advocated a revision of the treaty.

In reply to this report the Canadian minister of finance made a defense of the policy of his province. The report took up in detail the several causes of dissatisfaction mentioned by the Americans.[1]

Besides the report of 1862 and the Canadian reply, there was a brief report made in April, 1864, from the committee on commerce. This also was the work of Mr. Ward, and really formed a supplement to his report of 1862. It formed the basis of the final struggle in the House over the abrogation of the treaty. The final paragraph recommended—

"That the President be authorized to give notice to the government of Great Britain that it is the intention of the government of the United States to terminate the reciprocity treaty made with Great Britain for the British North American provinces, ... unless a new convention shall be concluded between the two governments, by which the provisions shall be abrogated or so modified as to be mutually satisfactory to both governments; and that the President be also authorized to appoint three commissioners, by and with the advice and consent of the Senate, for the revision of the treaty, and to confer with other commissioners duly authorized therefor, whenever it shall appear to be the wish of the government of Great Britain to negotiate a new treaty between the two governments and the people of both countries, based upon true principles of reciprocity, and for the removal of existing difficulties."[2]

The report was accompanied by a joint resolution[3] embodying the substance of the recommendations of the committee on commerce. This joint resolution

---

[1] "Report of Minister of Finance upon the Report of Committee of Commerce of House of Representatives." March, 1862.

[2] "Reports of Committees." First Session Thirty-eighth Congress, 1863-4, Vol. I, No. 39.

[3] *Congressional Globe*, First Session, Thirty-eighth Congress, 1863-4, p. 1387.

was the subject of the debate in the House upon the abrogation of the treaty on May 18–19 and May 24–26. In this debate Mr. Ward acted as the leader of the friends of the treaty, making two able speeches in its favor, at the opening and closing of the debate respectively. He was supported by Isaac N. Arnold of Illinois, Thomas D. Eliot of Massachusetts, John V. L. Pruyn and Thomas T. Davis of New York, Rufus P. Spaulding of Ohio, J. C. Allen of Illinois, and L. D. M. Sweat of Maine. Justin S. Morrill of Vermont led the opposition, assisted by Frederick A. Pike of Maine, Francis W. Kellogg of Michigan, and Portus Baxter of Vermont. The merits of the debate were certainly with the friends of the treaty, for the opposition contented itself with denunciation of the treaty, and with invectives against the unfriendly policy of Great Britain.

Mr. Arnold, of Illinois, offered an amendment to the resolution proposed by the committee on commerce. This amendment authorized the President to use his discretion in abrogating the treaty in case of a failure in the negotiation of a revised treaty satisfactory to both governments.[1] Mr. Morrill of Vermont proposed an amendment in the nature of a substitute for the resolution of the committee on commerce. This provided for an unconditional abrogation of the treaty.[2]

On May 26, 1864. the House voted upon the three propositions before it. Mr. Arnold's amendment was defeated by a vote of 54 to 97. Mr. Morrill's substitute met the same fate by a vote of 74 to 82. The

---

[1] *Congressional Globe*, First Session, Thirty-eighth Congress, 1863–4, p. 2455.

[2] Same, p. 2364.

original resolution of the committee was finally post-
poned to the second Tuesday in December by a vote
of 77 to 72, after having been read a third time. A
motion to lay the resolution on the table failed by a
vote of 73 to 76.[1]

On December 13, 1864, the House took up the joint
resolution and passed it by a vote of 85 to 57, forty
members not voting. A good deal of party manœu-
vering preceded the final vote, the opposition led by
Mr. Morrill attempting to substitute a resolution for
unconditional abrogation.

The second great debate upon the resolution occur-
red in the Senate in January, 1865.

On December 14, 1864, the Senate received the
resolution from the House and referred it, after a
short debate, to the committee on foreign relations.
Senator Grimes of Iowa moved that the resolution be
referred to the committee on commerce, as "it refers
to commercial relations existing between this country
and the provinces of Great Britain." In reply Senator Sumner said that "every question of commerce
between the two countries, even if it is the subject of
negotiation, must be referred to the committee on
commerce, and you may as well dismiss your committee on foreign relations." Finally the resolution
was referred to the committee on foreign affairs.

This action of the Senate indicates the way in which
the measure was to be considered. Instead of treat-
ing the matter as one of commercial relations, the Senate proceeded to act upon it as a political measure.

[1] House debate, *Congressional Globe*, First Session, Thirty-eighth
Congress, Part III, May 18, 2333-38; May 19, 2361-71; May 24, 2452-
56; May 25, 2476-84; May 26, 2502-09.

[2] *Congressional Globe*, Second Session, Thirty-eighth Congress, 1864-
65, p. 35.

As I have already said, this was the attitude of the opponents of the treaty throughout the whole discussion.

The committee on foreign relations, through Mr. Sumner, reported an amendment to the original resolution, providing for the unconditional abrogation of the treaty.[1]

The debate upon the amendment lasted through the two days, January 11–12, 1865, and ended with the passage of the measure on the latter day by a vote of 33 to 8.

The debate was long and thorough. The opposition excelled in the brilliancy of its speakers. Charles Sumner, John Sherman, Jacob Collamer and Solomon Foot of Vermont, Zachariah Chandler of Michigan, James R. Doolittle of Wisconsin, Nathan A. Farwell of Maine, and John Conness of California, spoke for the abrogation. John P. Hale of New Hampshire, Alexander Ramsey of Minnesota, Timothy O. Howe of Wisconsin, and Thomas A. Hendricks of Indiana opposed the abrogation.

The prestige of distinguished services was certainly with the opposition, but the strength of solid argument rested with the friends of the treaty. Said Senator John P. Hale, in concluding his speech[2] in favor of a revision of the treaty:

"If the treaty is imperfect and needs amendment, that [the proposed amendment for revision] is the true, statesmanlike, Christian way of annulling it. . . . But if, on the other hand, smarting as we now are under what we believe and feel to be injustice on the part of these colonies, we resort to this legislation at this time, in this hour, under such impulses, it will tend to increase and intensify all the

[1] *Congressional Globe,* Second Session, Thirty-eighth Congress, pp. 71 and 95–97.

[2] *Congressional Globe,* Second Session, Thirty-eighth Congress, 1864–65. Part I. pp. 204–06.

bad feelings that have unhappily existed; will, in fact, retard, if not render utterly impossible any future progress in the line of reciprocity between these two countries."

A brief quotation from the speech of an opponent will indicate the spirit with which the treaty was attacked. Said Senator Jacob Collamer of Vermont:

" I acknowledge that I have some prejudice against this treaty. I am a little situated as my old neighbor Judge Chipman was when he was called upon to testify whether a certain witness was a man of truth. He said he was not. He was then asked, 'Sir, are you not conscious that you labor under a prejudice against that man?' He answered, 'I think it likely that I am, I have detected him stealing two or three times.' "[1]

Justice to the opponents of the treaty requires it to be said that the quotation just cited is an extreme example of the opinions of that party. The address of the late Hannibal Hamlin before the commercial convention at Detroit, in July, 1865, indicates the opinions of the more moderate opponents of the treaty. He said:

"I was educated in the school of free trade,—not free trade in slices. I affirm that that is the most obnoxious system of legislation that can be devised by man. I am for free trade. . . . . But what do I mean by free trade? Not that system which selects a few articles and makes them entirely free, rendering it necessary that you shall impose additional revenue upon other articles in order to make up for the deficiency. That is free trade in slices, and it cannot be defended upon any principle of political economy ever enunciated by any man."[2]

On January 16, 1865, the House concurred in the amendment of the Senate to the joint resolution. The resolution, as finally passed, proposed an unconditional abrogation of the treaty, "as it is no longer

[1] *Congressional Globe*, Second Session, Thirty-eighth Congress, 1864-65, Part I. p. 210. For debates January 11-12, 1865, pp. 204-13 and pp. 222-34.

[2] See pp. 59-61. The speech is given in the "Proceedings" of the convention, p. 100.

for the interests of the United States to continue the same in force."[1] This resolution received the approval of the President, January 18, 1865.[2] The treaty terminated March 17, 1866.

Delegates from Canada, New Brunswick and Nova Scotia arrived at Washington January 24, 1866, and remained there until February 6. The delegates were A. J. Galt, minister of finance, and W. P. Howland, postmaster-general, representing Canada; A. J. Smith, attorney-general of New Brunswick, and W. A. Henry, attorney-general of Nova Scotia. After many days discussion the negotiations terminated unsuccessfully.[3]

The unsuccessful attempt at renewal made by the provincial delegates was followed by an equally unsuccessful attempt to continue a semblance of reciprocity by means of legislation. During the last week in February a bill with such an object in view, was introduced in the House by Mr. Justin S. Morrill, chairman of the committee on ways and means, and was debated on March 6, 7, 9, 12. But even a bill, which offered terms that could only be called recip-

---

[1] *Congressional Globe*, Second Session Thirty-eighth Congress, Part 1, p. 277.

The best speeches in favor of the revision of the treaty, delivered in the Senate, were those of John P. Hale, *Congressional Globe*, Second Session, Thirty-eighth Congress, pp. 204–06, and Timothy O. Howe, *Globe*, pp 211–13, and pp. 226–29. These two speeches, with the two speeches of Mr. Ward, delivered in the House May 18 and 26, 1864 (see p. 22), state clearly and forcibly the views of the friends of the treaty.

[2] "Statutes at Large," Second Session, Thirty-eighth Congress, p. 566.

[3] "Canada and the States," Sir E. W. Watkin, pp. 405–13. Contains report of the delegates, their proposals, the counter proposals of the committee of Ways and Means, and finally the reply of the delegates.

rocal by "political" license, had no chance of success
in the existing state of opinion in Congress and in
the country.   Mr. Morrill set the keynote of the debate when he said in his speech at the opening of the
discussion, that)"the treaty was an ill-omened one
from the start, having been first extorted from us by
the armed raid upon our fishermen in 1852, made by
the combined armaments of the provinces, and led on
by the imperial government; and secondly, won from
us by the delusion that favor would beget fraternity.
We are too old to be again deluded, and being quite
able to withstand a bite, we shall be less likely to
yield to a growl."[1] A few believed that the wiser
policy was to cultivate friendly relations with the
provinces, but the majority thought otherwise, and
the bill failed to pass.   One of the minority said
during the debate that—

"He would not have risen, ... if he had not voted last
year, with others, for an abrogation of the reciprocity treaty, and
if he did not see now, from the tendencies and sympathies of the
House, that the moment the bill passed from the hands of the committee of the whole it would receive its final death blow. He did not
believe that there would have been thirty votes obtained in this
House last year for the abrogation of the reciprocity treaty with
Canada, but for the explicit understanding that some sort of reciprocity in trade would be forthwith re-established, either through
the treaty-making power, or through the legislative power of the
government. The people of the United States were ground down
by the internal revenue taxation, and he had not felt at liberty to
let the reciprocity treaty stand, without being at liberty to make
some sort of bargain with the people of Canada, that whatever our
internal revenues might be, the same would be levied, either by
them or by us, on our imports from them. It was exclusively on that
understanding that he had voted for the abrogation of the treaty.
And he now saw in the additional claims of those who repre-
sented the lumber interests, and the coal and other interests of the
country, that advantage was to be taken of the present opportu-

---

[1] *Congressional Globe*, 1865–66, March 6, 1866, p. 1210.

nity, and that never again were we to have reciprocity with
the neighboring provinces. . . . . If that were to be so, he
never should regret any vote that he gave in his life as he would
regret his vote of last winter, to abrogate the treaty. He had
given it with the understanding that it should be substantially
renewed,"[1]

Why was the treaty abrogated? Charles Francis
Adams,[2] minister to Great Britain, wrote February
2, 1865, to Secretary Seward that in his belief "all
these measures [for abrogation] were the result
rather of a strong political feeling than of any commercial considerations. I should not disguise the
fact of the prevalence of great irritation in consequence of the events that had taken place in Canada;
neither should I conceal my regret, as it seemed to
me to be one of the cardinal points of our policy, both
in a political and commercial sense, to maintain the
most friendly relations with the whole population
along our northern border."

Senator Wilson, of Massachusetts, said in the Senate, January 12, 1865:

"When this treaty was negotiated it was believed to be for the
general interests of the country, and in Massachusetts it was especially believed to be for our fishing, manufacturing, commercial
and railroad interests. I have ever been in favor of the treaty, and
up to this time could never have been induced to vote against it. I
am not clear now that it is not for the interests of the state I in part
represent to let it stand. I am inclined to think it is for our interest
that the treaty should stand as it now does. For the interests of the
whole country I am of the opinion that it ought to be modified or
perhaps abrogated."[3]

---

[1] *Congressional Globe.* Part II, 1865-66. March 7, 1866, p. 1250.
For the debate see *Globe* 1865-66, February 27, March 6, 7, 9, 12,
1866, pp. 1867, 1210-20, 1241-51, 1297-1302, 1333-43.

[2] "House Executive Documents," First Session Thirty-ninth
Congress, Vol. I, Part I, p. 111.

[3] *Congressional Globe,* Second Session Thirty-eighth Congress, Part
I, p. 233.

A convention composed of boards of trade and
chambers of commerce of the United States and
British North American provinces met at Detroit
July 11–14, 1865, by invitation of the local board of
trade, to protest against the abrupt termination of
the reciprocity treaty. This convention was composed of business men and others, representing the
leading commercial bodies of the country. Representatives were present from New York, Michigan,
Massachusetts, Maine, Illinois, Ohio, Canada (west),
Prince Edward Island, Pennsylvania, Nova Scotia,
Canada (east), Wisconsin, Minnesota, Missouri, New
Brunswick. Among these were Lyman Tremain,
John V. L. Pruyn, late chancellor of the University
of the State of New York, and Martin Townsend, of
New York; Frederick Farley, afterward president of
the national board of trade; John Welsh, afterward
minister to Great Britain; A. G. Cattell and William
Elder, of Pennsylvania; Joseph S. Ropes, James E.
Converse and W. W. Greenough, of Massachusetts;
Morrison R. Waite, afterward chief justice of the
supreme court of Ohio; James F. Joy, of Michigan,
and others. The convention came "to substantial
unanimity and they united in urging upon the government at Washington the great importance of
immediately opening negotiations with the British
government for a new arrangement, at the least as
liberal on both sides as the one about to expire had
been, and as much broader as should appear practi-
cable. Their action was approved by every board
of trade and chamber of commerce in the country
taking any interest in the matter; it was disapproved,
so far as we ever heard, by none."[1]

[1] "Proceedings of the Commercial Convention held in Detroit
July 11–14, 1865." Detroit, 1865. I am indebted to the son of the

And yet Mr. Larned, in his report[1] in 1871 declares that the treaty was "justly abrogated in 1866 with the very general sanction of public opinion in the country." Do the opinions of a minister to England, of a senator of the United States and of a convention of representative business men, count for nothing?[2]

THE WORKING OF THE TREATY.

Of the effect of the treaty upon the commerce of the two countries Senator Sumner said in a speech delivered in the Senate in January, 1865, in favor of its abrogation :

"This has increased immensely, but it is difficult to say how much of this increase is due to the treaty and how much is due to the natural growth of population and the facilities of transportation in both countries. If it could be traced exclusively, or in any large measure, to the treaty, it would be an element not to be disregarded. But it does not follow, from the occurrence of this measure *after* the treaty that it is on *account* of the treaty. *Post hoc ergo propter hoc* is too loose a rule for our government on the present occasion."[3]

late Joseph C. Bates, of Boston, for the loan of a scrap-book containing clippings from newspaper editorials written by Mr. Bates. I quote above from one of these editorials.

[1]"House Executive Documents," 1870-71, Vol. VIII, No. 94, p. 6.

[2]It is difficult to determine the real attitude of the principal parties in regard to reciprocity. The bill providing for reciprocity with Canada, passed in the House in 1848, was reported by a Whig committee and passed in a House containing a Whig majority. On the other hand the same bill failed in the Democratic Senate, and the opposition of another Democratic Senate threatened to cause the collapse of the negotiations in 1854. The other attempts to bring about reciprocity by legislation, and the first negotiation of a treaty was carried out by Democrats. Furthermore the support of the policy of reciprocity in 1864-65 came from the Democrats, while the Republicans opposed it. Throughout the period the slavery question, or questions connected with it, determined the attitude of parties upon questions of less pressing importance.

Congressional Globe, 1864-65, p. 206. January 11, 1865.

Before beginning a discussion of the effects of the treaty three points must be insisted upon: (1) In a discussion based upon statistics, it must be remembered that the figures used are not mathematically accurate. Therefore conclusions drawn from them are subject to some qualification, although it is not intended to deal with distinctions so fine that they are likely to be affected by occasional inaccuracies in the details of the statistics. (2) The treaty was only one of several causes at work at the same time upon the commerce of the two countries. The increase of population, the improvement in the means of transportation through the building of canals and railroads, and the development of manufacturing industries, were acting upon trade as never before in the history of the world. (3) The working of the treaty was disturbed by two economic events, the crisis of 1857 and the civil war of 1861–65.

In sixty-four years, 1821 to 1885, the total trade (exports and imports combined) between the United States and the British provinces, increased from $2,500,495 to $88,214,020. The trade[1] by decades has been as follows:

1821	$2,500,495	1861	$51,245,224
1831	4,926,747	1871	59,727,723
1841	8,624,750	1881	87,030,472
1851	19,543,469		

The increase of trade[2] by decades has been as follows:

1821–1831	$2,426,252	1851–1861	31,701,755
1831–1841	3,698,003	1861–1871	8,482,499
1841–1851	10,918,719	1871–1881	27,302,749

[1] That is the amount of the total trade in each tenth year.

[2] That is, the amount of increase in the total trade in 1831 over 1821, 1841 over 1831, so on. For the statistics of trade from 1821–85 see Appendix, p. 59–61.

These figures show that the trade was comparatively small up to 1840: that the decade from 1841–
51 witnessed the beginning of the great development
of the last fifty years; that the decade from 1851 to
1861 was marked by the greatest increase of trade
which has taken place down to 1881; and that the
decade from 1861–71 saw the smallest increase since
that of 1831–41. The decade 1851–61 included a portion of the period influenced by the reciprocity treaty,
while that of 1861–71 covered the period of its abrogation, and of the disturbance caused by the civil
war.

For the twelve years of the continuance of the
treaty the total trade year by year was as follows:

1855	$49,000,000	1861	$50,000,000
1856	57,000,000	1862	48,000,000
1857	49,000,006	1863	46,000,000
1858	37,000,000	1864	?? ......
1859	45,000,000	1865	60,000,000
1860	48,000,000	1866	75,000,000

These figures show the effect of the treaty very
clearly. The total trade for the last year before the
treaty was $34,899,544, while for the first year of
the treaty it was $57,041,594,[1] an increase of $22,
142,050 for the first year under the treaty compared with an increase of $9,184,896 during three
years (1850–53) before the treaty. Under the favorable conditions furnished by the reciprocity treaty,
the trade increased more than twice as much in one
year as it had in there years without the treaty.

---

[1] I take the year 1856 because it was the first full year, the
treaty going into effect March 16, 1855.

This increased trade continued with the usual fluctuations during the continuance of the treaty:

Total Trade under Treaty of 1854.	1858...................	$37,995,673
	1860...................	49,444,195
	1862...................	48,888,897
	1865...................	60,533,561

Total Trade before the Treaty.	1844...................	$8,181,618
	1846...................	9,344,150
	1848...................	12,029,122
	1850...................	16,788,141

Total Trade after the Treaty.	1867...................	$50,283,464
	1868...................	48,905,613
	1870...................	58,134,775
	1872...................	70,088,925

Total Trade under the Treaty of 1871.[1]	1875...................	$76,508,092
	1877...................	75,732,919
	1879...................	69,677,055
	1882...................	103,976,742

An examination of the preceding figures shows that the abrogation of the treaty did not seriously disturb the amount of trade. At least the effect was not permanent; for the trade had begun to recover before the negotiation of the treaty of 1871. Of course a considerable portion of this increase may have been due, and undoubtedly was due, to the natural increase of business, the result of the increase of wealth and of improvements in production and transportation, but is it not likely that the permanent effects of the treaty had something to do with this increase? May not the influence of the treaty have developed a trade which continued after its expiration? It seems probable to me, and if true, gives to the reciprocity treaty of 1854 an importance which has never been recognized.

Besides the effect of the treaty, as shown by the increase of trade, the amount of the imports into the

---

[1] Went into effect July 1, 1873.

3

United States for 1866 (the last year of the operation of the treaty), $48,528,628, gives ground for the conjecture that this unusually large quantity was due to the desire of business men to profit as much as possible by the treaty. There are two reasons for this conjecture: (1) because the fiscal year ending June 30, 1866, was not coincident with the existence of the treaty, which terminated March 17, 1866. Consequently this excessive importation was the work of less than nine months. (2) This amount of importation was not again reached until 1882, when $50,775,-581 of goods were imported from the Dominion of Canada.[1]

Mr. Larned, in his "Report on Trade with the British North American Provinces," says that—

"To a remarkable extent our present trade with the provinces is what might be characterized as a pure *commerce of convenience,* incident merely to the economical distribution of products which are common to both countries. We exchange with them almost equal quantities of the cereals, and almost equal quantities, on an average of flour. Except so far as concerns the barley that we buy and the Indian corn that we sell to them, this trade orignates on neither side in any necessity, but is chiefly a matter of simple convenience, of economy in carriage, or of diversification in the qualities of grain. Similarly and for the like reasons we exchange with them about equal quantities of coal. We sell them a certain quantity of hides and skins, and buy half that quantity of the same articles back from them. On the other hand, they sell us provisions and wool and buy our provisions and wool to half the amount in return. Not less than one-third, probably, of the trade now carried on between the United States and the neighboring provinces is of that character, and the fact that it is kept up with so little diminution, notwithstanding the imposition of duties on both sides of the frontier, is significant of the value of the advantages that are found in it."[2]

[1] Another reason for the large imports in 1865-66 has been suggested to me by Professor Taussig: high prices in the United States due to paper money inflation, while yet there was gold in the country for export.

"House Executive Documents," 1870-71, Vol. VIII, No. 94, p. 15.

This "commerce of convenience" is natural
enough when we consider the geograpical relations
of the two countries. The British provinces are by
nature divided into groups bearing a closer relation
to adjacent portions of the United States than to the
other parts of the British possessions. The maritime
provinces are more intimately connected with the
neighboring New England states than with the Canadas, Ontario and Quebec, while the Canadas in their
turn find their easiest communication with the mid-
dle states of the Union. This grouping of the various
provinces has received still greater emphasis by the
rapid development of the western provinces of the
dominion, a development hardly begun at the time
of the reciprocity treaty.

The same reason for a "commerce of convenience"
appears when we examine the economic relations of
the two countries. On this point Goldwin Smith
says:

"Let any one scan the economical map of the North American
continent, with its adjacent waters, mark its northern zone abound-
ing in minerals, in bituminous coal, in lumber, in fish, as well as
in special farm products, brought in the north to hardier perfection,
of all of which the southern people have need; then let him look to
its southern regions, the natural products of which, as well as the
manufactures produced in its wealthy centres of industry, are needed
by the people of the northern zone; he will see that the continent
is an economic whole, and that to run a customs line athwart it and
try to sever its members from each other, is to wage a desperate war
against nature."[1]

Furthermore a "commerce of convenience" is not
the only necessary commerce between the United
States and the provinces. The maritime provinces
have lumber, bituminous coal and fish which they

---

[1]"Canada and the Canadian Question." Goldwin Smith. London, 1891. pp. 283-84.

desire to sell, and New England is anxious to buy.
The Canadas, Ontario and Quebec, produce barley,
eggs, and other farm products; horses, cattle and
lumber, for the sale of which they look to New York
and other neighboring states. All the provinces want
to get American manufactures as well as the products
of a more southerly climate in return.

The argument of the opponents of reciprocity, that
there cannot be profitable commerce between Canada
and the United States, because their products are the
same, is not true. The United States includes regions
and productions almost tropical. Canada has bituminous coal, which is needed in parts of the United
States, and an abundance of nickel, of which there
is but little in the United States. Canada has a vast
supply of lumber, and the United States needs all that
it can get. Both countries produce barley, but the
Canadian barley is the best for making beer.[1]

"High as the tariff wall between Canada and the
United State is, trade has climbed over it." In 1889
the trade between Canada and the United States was
greater than that between Canada and any other
country, and nearly as great as that between Canada
and all the countries in the world put together.[2]

The treaty was intended to provide for the exchange of natural products between the two countries, and with very few exceptions these products
were in the crudest possible condition, just as they
were taken from the field or forest, or dug from the
soil, or obtained from the sea. They were raw ma-

---

[1] "The Canadian Question," p. 287-88.

[2] 1889—Canada and Great Britain, $38,105,126 exports, $42,249,555
imports; Canada and the United States, $48,522,404 exports, $56,-
368,990 imports.

terials in the fullest sense of the word, and may be grouped under five heads: products of the mine, of the forest, of the sea, animal products and agricultural produce.

Products of the Mine.—

Coal, ores of metals of all kinds; stone or marble, unwrought; grindstones, wrought and unwrought; slate; gypsum, ground and unground.

Products of the Forest.—

Timber and lumber, round, hewed. sawed; firewood; pitch, tar and turpentine.

Products of the Sea.—

Fish and fish products.

Animal products.—

Animals of all kinds; meats, fresh, smoked, salted; hides, furs, skins, undressed; poultry, eggs, butter, cheese, tallow, lard, horns, manures, pelts, wool.

Agricultural products.—

Grain, flour and breadstuffs; cotton-wool, seeds and vegetables; dried and undried fruits; plants, shrubs and trees; rice, broom-corn and bark; flax, hemp and tow; tobacco, unmanufactured.

In this list a few are included which may, perhaps, not be fairly classed as raw products. For instance, flour, smoked and salted meats, dried fruits; timber and lumber, round, hewn and sawed. But these form a small number compared with the total number provided for by the treaty.

The trade for the ten years, 1853–1863, may be summarized as follows :[1]

Products of the Mine (imported into United States).—

1853...	$ 58,400
1856.............................	84,228
1860.............................	318,537
1863.............................	1,114,831

Products of the Forest.—

1853.............................	2,589,898
1856.............................	3,345,284
1860.............................	4,019,278
1863.............................	3,679,559

Products of the Sea.—

1853.............................	73,422
1856.............................	140,948.
1860.............................	185,873
1863.............................	957,166

Animal Products.—

1853.............................	1,107,870
1856.............................	2,375,388
1860.............................	3,557,912
1863.............................	3,133,463

Agricultural Products.—

1853.............................	4,949,576
1856.............................	11,864,836
1860.............................	10,013,799
1863.............................	7,005,826

The largest imports before the treaty were of agricultural produce, and in 1863 they remained still the largest, having also made the largest gain— about three millions—during the decade. The second place, both in 1853 and in 1863, belonged to the products of the forest, the gain, however, being inferior to that made by animal products. Animal

[1] For detailed statistics see Appendix, pp. 63–64.

products occupied the third place at the beginning
and the ending of the period, while the gain was
superior to that made by the products of the forest.
The fourth and fifth places were held by fish products and the products of the mine, the latter dis-
placing the former between 1853 and 1863.

Turning now to the imports from the United
States into Canada, we have the following figures :

Products of the Mine (imported into Canada).—

1853	$ 126,586
1856	488,984
1860	406,688
1863	647,965

Products of the Forest.—

1853	66,620
1856	302,904
1860	137,392
1863	134,281

Products of the Sea.—

1853	383,436
1856	411,716
1860	227,112
1863	281,023

Animal Products.—

1853	570,587
1856	2,896,858
1860	1,679,912
1863	3,050,294

Agricultural Products.—

1853	668,113
1856	3,809,112
1860	4,603,114
1863	8,137,447[1]

As is the case of the United States imports, the
largest item in the Canadian in 1853 was that of

---

[1] For detailed statistics see Appendix, pp. 63-64.

agricultural produce, and this proportion remained the same in 1863, the increase being remarkable— about seven and a-half millions.[1] The second place was held by animal products, both at the beginning and at the end of the period, the gain also being next in amount to that of agricultural produce. Products of the sea occupied the third place at the beginning, but had fallen to fourth place at the end, with the additional disgrace of having had a decrease instead of a gain during the ten years. Products of the mine rose from fourth place to third from 1853–1863, making a gain in amount next to that of animal products. Finally products of the forest held and retained the fifth place.

The following figures show the amount of the trade in a few leading articles:[2]

Animals (imported into United States.)—

		INCREASE.
1862	$1,532,957	
1865	5,503,318	$3,970,361

Barley.—

| 1862 | 1,095,443 | |
| 1865 | 4,093,202 | 2,997,759 |

Timber.—

| 1862 | 2,526,658 | |
| 1865 | 4,515,626 | 1,988,968 |

Oats.—

| 1862 | 634,176 | |
| 1865 | 2,216,722 | 1,582,546 |

[1] These figures are liable to considerable qualification, being at best rough estimates. See Appendix, p. 63, note.

[2] The figures are taken from the reports of the Minister of Finance of Canada and of the Secretary of the Treasury of the United States. Separate tables for articles included in the treaty are given for Canada, 1858–1863; and for the United States, July 1, 1861, and June 30, 1866.

Wool.—

		INCREASE.
1862	569,839	
1865	1,527,275	957,436

Meats.—

1862	128,935	
1865	850,328	721,393

Coal.—

1862	614,556	
1865	1,210,004	595,448

Grain, all kinds (imported into Canada).—

1858	2,078,464	
1863	5,062,610	3,984,146

Meats.—

1858	544,366	
1863	1,238,923	694,557

Coal.—

1858	242,700	
1863	548,846	306,146

Animals.—

1858	240,186	
1863	520,835	280,649

Hides.—

1858	125,000	
1863	384,951	259,951

Cheese.—

1858	90,045	
1863	294,327	204,282

Wool.—

1858	11,101	
1863	208,858	197,757

Flour.—

1858	750,580	
1863	898,029	147,449

These figures show that the articles of first importance on the side of the United States were those of
animal products, and barley, timber, oats, wool,
meats and coal: on the side of Canada grain occupied the first place, followed by meats, coal, animals,
hides, cheese, wool and flour. If barley and oats
were combined in the United States imports as they
are in the Canadian under the single head of grain,
they would take the first place, and grain would
then be the largest import into both countries. Of
course these figures are not for the same years and
some slight allowance must be made for the varying
conditions of the two periods. The period 1858-1863
covers only a part of the war period, while the years
1862-1865 are wholly included in that period. As
was said at the beginning of the discussion, the
course of trade under the treaty was disturbed by
two great economic events, so that no certain in-
ference may be drawn from the actual course of
trade. Moreover, the whole period of the treaty
was almost too short to allow sound conclusions to
be drawn from the figures representing its progress.

The trade between the United States and the other
British provinces from 1849-1863 can be summarized
as follows: the figures are taken from a table of leading exports to British provinces other than Canada
from 1849 1863.[1]

Wheat.—

1849	332,765
1853	208,956
1856	268,959
1860	90,049
1863	110,333

See Appendix, p. 66.

Wheat Flour.—

1849..	1,518,922
1853	784,498
1856	3,120,787
1860	3,044,243
1863	4,420,748

Indian Corn.—

1849	126,791
1853	105,404
1856	136,774
1860	85,915
1863	131,552

Meal, Corn and Rye.—

1849	625,691
1853	135,040
1856	631,959
1860	206,881
1863	286,238

The most noticeable features in these figures are the decline in the amount of exports in wheat, corn and rye meal, and the large increase in wheat flour. The population of the maritime provinces was small and their resources were undeveloped. New England had not yet come to need the raw materials of which the provinces possessed an abundance, and therefore the resources were not developed during the continuance of the treaty. These reasons probably explain to a considerable extent the failure of the treaty to produce a greater effect upon the trade. The remarkable increase in the export of wheat-flour from a million and a-half to nearly four millions and a-half— may be explained by the fact that the United States imported wheat and re-exported it in the form of wheat-flour.

The following figures show the relative amount of trade between the United States and Canada, and between the United States and the other British provinces:

UNITED STATES IMPORTS.[1]

	Canada.	Other Provinces.
1850	4,285,470	1,358,992
1853	5,278,116	2,272,602.
1856	17,488,197	3,822,224
1860	18,861,673	4,989,708
1862	15,253,152	4,046,843

UNITED STATES EXPORTS.[1]

	Canada.	Other Provinces.
1850	5,930,821	3,618,214
1853	7,829,099	5,311,543
1856	20,883,241	8,146,108
1860	14,083,114	8,623,214
1862	12,842,504	8,236,611

The proportion of trade with these two groups, the Canadas and the maritime provinces, Nova Scotia, New Brunswick, Prince Edward Island and Newfoundland, seems to have been little affected by the treaty. The imports from Canada were three times as large as those from the maritime provinces in 1850 and in 1862. The exports, too, bore about the same proportion to each other in both years, those to Canada being somewhat less than twice as large as those to the maritime provinces. The effect of the treaty appears much more striking in the Canada trade than in that to the maritime provinces. From 1853-1856 the imports from Canada were more than trebled, while those from the maritime provinces do not double. The exports to Canada during the same period nearly treble, while those to the other pro-

---

[1] Statistics of comparative amounts of exports 1849–1863; of imports 1850–1863, Appendix p. 65.

vinces again do not double. The total trade between
the United States and Canada was in—

    1853...........................13,107,215
    1856...........................38,371,438

The total trade between the United States and the
maritime provinces was in—

    1853........................... 7,584,145
    1856...........................11,968,532

During the discussion over the abrogation of the
treaty the common assertion was that the Unite l
States allowed the principal Canadian exports to
enter free of duty, while Canada, on the other hand,
imposed a duty upon exports of manufactured goods
of the United States. The following figures show
the amounts of free and dutiable goods imported into
the United States and Canada in several different
years from 1850-1862:

UNITED STATES IMPORTS.[1]

	Free.	*Dutiable.*
1850.......	787,599	4,856,863
1853......	1,418,250	6,132,468
1856......	20,488,697	821,724
1860......	23,180,971	690,411
1862......	18,770, 737	529,258

CANADIAN IMPORTS.

	Free.	*Dutiable.*
1850.......	791,128	5,803,732
1853........	1,125,565	10,656,582
1856........	9,933,586	12,770,923
1860........	8,746,799	8,526,230
1862........	19,044,374	6,128,783

Of the United States imports the amount of free
importation increased from $787,599 in 1850 to

---

[1]Comparative amount of free and dutiable goods, 1850-1863,
Appendix, p. 64.

\$23,180,971 in 1860, while that of dutiable goods decreased from \$6,132,468 in 1853 to \$529,258 in 1862. Of Canadian imports the free importations increased from \$791,128 in 1850 to \$19,044,374 in 1862, while the dutiable goods remained about the same, amounting to \$5,803,732 in 1850 and to \$6,128,-783 in 1862. An actual increase in the amount of dutiable goods occurred from 1853-1856. The figures for these years were as follows:

1853	10,656,582
1854	13,449,341
1855	11,449,472
1856	12,770,923

The amounts gradually declined, until in 1862 it reached the lowest amount of the twelve years, 1851-1862 inclusive. This large amount of dutiable goods may have been the result of the better trade relations established between the two countries by the treaty, although the largest amount of dutiable imports during the period 1850-62 was in 1854, the year before the treaty went into operation. The amount of dutiable goods imported into the United States, therefore, declined from about \$5,000,000 in 1850 until it reached the small amount of \$529,000 in 1862—not only a smaller amount absolutely, but, of course, a much smaller amount in proportion to the increased amount of trade. The amount of dutiable goods imported into Canada, on the other hand, increased absolutely, although the amount bore a smaller proportion to the total trade. The increase in free goods was about the same in both countries, except for the years, 1856 and 1860, when the increase of United States imports was much greater than that of Canadian imports.

The treaty of 1854 applied almost exclusively to natural products, leaving manufactures upon the same foundations upon which they had rested before the treaty. Curiously enough, however, the question of manufactures played an important part in the abrogation of the treaty. The one really serious complaint made by the opponents of the treaty against it, and admitted even by its friends, was the violation of the spirit of the treaty by the province of Canada by the increase of the provincial tariff on articles not included in the treaty. The importance of this action of Canada will be understood when it is remembered that the population of Canada formed the largest portion of the population of the provinces, being 2,500,000 out of a total of 3,253,000. The Canadian trade, therefore, formed by far the largest part of the trade of the British provinces, that of the remainder, containing only about 700,000 inhabitants, being relatively unimportant. With these other provinces there was no dissatisfaction during the existence of the treaty. Trade with them was a local matter of interest only to the people of New England. Their slow development had not in 1860 made clear the importance of their natural resources. Hence the arguments for a closer union with the maritime provinces, so prevalent to-day, had not yet made their appearance.

The increase of the Canadian tariff was a part of the same policy which had dictated the negotiation of the reciprocity treaty, a policy having for its object the development of the resources of the provinces. To carry out this policy the Canadian government embarked on a system of internal improvements destined to develop their resources. Canals were built and improved, the navigation of the St. Lawrence was improved, and railroads were constructed. The idea of the government seems to have been to direct the carrying trade of the new western states of the Union from the railroads and canals of New York to Canadian canals and railroads. The negotiation of the reciprocity treaty gave a favorable opportunity for such a scheme.

These improvements in transportation were undertaken by the government and were mainly dependent upon subsidies and municipal bonds. No doubt the object of these works was as much political as commercial, the desire of the Canadian statesmen having been to consolidate the separate provinces and by an increase in the material wealth of the people to remove all discontent, which from the situation of the country, so easily developed into a desire for annexation to the United States.

Whatever the objects of the Canadian government, such works required large revenues for their completion.[1] Some increase of taxation became necessary. The easier method seemed to be to raise the tariff. This could not be done in the case of those articles included in the treaty, but could be done in the case of manufactured goods. This was done, and then arose the grievance of which the Americans so bitterly complained. From year to year, as a greater revenue was required, a higher tariff was imposed to the increasing disgust of the American manufacturer.

---

[1] "Canada and the States." Sir E. W. Watkin, p. 396.

The yearly changes from 1855–1859 in certain articles were as follows:

	1855.	1856.	1857.	1858.	1859.
Molasses	16%	11	11	18	30
Sugar (refined)	32	28	25	26½	40
Sugar (other)	27½	20	17½	21	30
Boots and Shoes	12½	14½	20	21	25
Harness	12½	17	20	21	25
Cotton Goods	12½	13½	15	15	20
Iron Goods	12½	18½	15	16	20
Silk Goods	12½	13½	15	17	20
Wool Good	12½	14	15	18	20[1]

The complaint of the Americans might have had a doubtful justification before the outbreak of the civil war, while the tariff of 1857 was in force. It could have none at all after the war tariffs came into existence. Even under the tariff of 1857, the tariff rate of the United States upon cotton and woolen goods was 24 per cent., 4 per cent. higher than the Canadian duty under the tariff of 1859. But the justification of the complaint does not rest with the comparative rate of duties. No formal complaint of a violation of the treaty was made by either party. The United States claimed that the treaty was made with the understanding that the tariff of Canada would remain the same as it had been at the conclusion of the treaty. But no clause to such an effect had been added to the treaty, and the United States could expect only a strict adhesion to the terms of the treaty.

---

[1]"House Executive Documents," 1859–1860, Vol. 13, No. 96, p. 10. Report of Israel T. Hatch on reciprocity treaty, March 28, 1860.

4

The following figures show the effect of the higher Canadian tariff upon the exports of manufactures from the United States:[1]

Cotton Manufactures.—

1858–59	$363,016
1862–63	64,495

Iron Manufactures, (except Pig Iron).

1858–59	761,619
1862–63	395,907

Boots and Shoes.—

1858–59	211,147
1862–63	22,860

Tobacco (Manufactured).—

1858–59	1,205,684
1862–63	76,026

House Furniture.—

1858-59	136,765
1862–63	66,718

Books.—

1858–59	154,034
1862–63	25,164

Hats.—

1858–59	116,150
1862–63	14,078

Musical Instruments.—

1858–59	104,534
1862–63	67,445

Unenumerated.—

1858–59	624,534
1862–63	401,227

These figures show a marked decrease in the exports of American manufactures to Canada from 1858 to 1863. Undoubtedly the increase in the rate

[1] For detailed statistics see Appendix, p. 66.

of the Canadian duties upon manufactured articles, was one of the causes of this falling off. Yet it must be remembered that the civil war broke out during the period, and that the effect which it produced upon the export of manufactures must have been considerable, especially in the case of the cotton manufactures. The needs of the United States increased, while its power of production diminished. This, of course, applied to all branches of production.

The following figures show the total amounts of the exports of American manufactures to Canada for the several years from 1858-1859 to 1862-1863.

1858–59..............................4,185,516
1859–60..............................3,548,114
1860–61..............................3,561,642
1861–62..............................2,596,930
1862–63..............................1,510,802

The privilege of free navigation of the river St. Lawrence, conferred by the fourth article of the treaty, had long been a subject of negotiation between the United States and Great Britain. The United States claimed a right of free navigation as "a riparian state of the upper waters of the river and of the lakes which feed it."[1] This privilege, granted temporarily in 1854, was given permanently by article XXVI of the treaty of 1871.

Besides the privilege of navigating the St. Lawrence, that of navigating those canals of Canada which formed the means of communication between the lakes and the sea, was granted by the fourth article of the treaty. This privilege proved a bone of contention between the two countries.

The interest of the United States in the navigation of the Canadian canals by its citizens upon the same

---

[1] Hall's "International Law," p. 118.

terms with Canadians related to the increasing needs of means of transportation from the grain producing states of the northwest to the sea-coast. The railroad system in the United States was still in the early stages of its development, the great through lines between the interior and the sea-coast not being completed until nearly ten years after the period of the reciprocity treaty. Great dependence was still made upon the canal system of the country, and many attempts were made for the improvement of the existing system. Doubtless, too, the blockade of the Mississippi during the civil war, thus cutting off one means of transportation to the sea, made the desire for any other possible avenue of communication with the sea stronger than it would otherwise have been.

The inadequacy of the existing means of transportation led, too, to a natural suspicion on the part of the producers of western grain that the owners of railroads and canals would use them for the furtherance of their own interests to the injury of the helpless producers. Thus early appeared the western hostility to railroads, which later influenced the legislation of many states.

Besides the western producers, anxious for a new avenue for the transportation of their products to market, a certain commercial element favored the continuance of free navigation, hoping thereby to profit by means of the larger trade which would be brought to their doors. This element seems to have been most active in the northern parts of New York, especially in Rochester, Oswego and Ogdensburg. Their expectation seems to have been to obtain a large share of the business of transportation from the west to the sea-coast. The course would naturally be, they thought, from the lakes through the Welland canal and Lake Ontario to their own wharves. Then they would profit greatly by such a trade.

But the interest of Canada in granting the privilege of navigating her canals to foreigners seems to have been clearly connected with the policy of internal development to which I have already referred. The canals were built for the benefit of Canada, and the grant of special privileges to Americans was expected to work towards that end. The diversion of a large part of the carrying trade from American canals and railroads would be a great gain to Canada and would surely cause such an increase of prosperity that all desire for annexation would die out of the minds of the people. Unfortuately the laws of nature were unfavorable to this scheme. For a good portion of each year the canals and rivers of Canada are frozen over, and consequently this new outlet for the surplus products of the west could have only a limited value. The attempt to thwart the laws of nature did not turn out as the projectors expected.

In the report of Hon. W. P. Howland, finance minister for Canada for the year 1862,[1] the results of this policy are examined. He says that "the movement of property on the provincial canals shows a steady increase."

On the Welland canal the movement was:

	Tons Property.	Tonnage of Vessels.
1859........	709,611	856,918
1860........	944,084	1,238,509
1861.......	1,020,483	1,327,672
1862........	1,243,774	1,476,842

[1] "House Executive Documents" 1863-1864, Vol. 9, No. 32, pp. 37-40. (Extract.)

On the St. Lawrence canals the movement was:

1859....... 631,769	765,636
1860....... 733,596	824,465
1861....... 886,908	1,009,469
1862....... 964,394	1,049,230

In 1860 the tolls on the St. Lawrence canals were abolished and those on the Welland canal reduced.

The report of the finance minister says upon this point, that though there has been an increase in the movement of property by the St. Lawrence route since the change, this increase must not be considered as due entirely to the remission of tolls. "The greatly increased production of cereals in the western states and the figures[1] presently introduced will show that in proportion to that increase, and to the whole volume of agricultural produce moved from Lakes Erie and Michigan to tide-water, we have not obtained so large a traffic since the removal of the tolls as we obtained prior to the adoption of that policy."

[1] Movement of American Breadstuffs.

Year.	Down the St. Lawrence.	Through Erie Canal.
1856	1,209,612 bus.	15,342,833 bus.
1857	1,930,280 "	10,601,532 "
1858	1,876,933 "	13,757,283 "
1859	1,988,759 "	10,371,966 "
1860	1,846,462 "	23,912,000 "
1861	3,103,153 "	34,427,800 "
1862	5,320,054 "	39,240,131 "

From this table it appears that for seven years the transportation of breadstuffs by the St. Lawrence route was—

1856...... 7. 3 per cent.	1860.... 7.16 per cent.
1857......15. 4 "	1861.... 8.26 "
1858......12.01 "	1862....11.04 "
1859......16.08 "	

From "House Executive Documents" First Session, Thirty-eighth Congress, Vol. IX, No. 32, p. 38. Extract from Finance Minister's Report for Canada, 1862.

While the Canadian canals failed to reap the
benefits expected from the reduction of tolls, the Erie
canal materially increased its tolls. This increase
amounted to an advance of seventy cents per ton on
wheat and flour from Buffalo to tide-water, and of
forty cents per ton from Oswego to tide-water.

The finance minister concludes from the results
of the free canal system that the policy has been
productive of benefit, neither to the producer nor to
the consumer of western breadstuffs. He says that
"it can be shown from trustworthy data that, in so
far as the actual cost of transportation is concerned,
western produce can be carried to tide-water much
cheaper by the St. Lawrence than by any competing
route." The cause of the failure of Canadian canals
to obtain a large proportion of the western trade is
due, in the opinion of the minister, to "the absence
of sufficient competition among forwarders engaged
in the St. Lawrence trade, to the financial relations
between shippers engaged in the western trade and
the capitalists of New York, and finally and chiefly,
to the lower rates of freights from New York to
Europe, occasioned by the greater competition at
that port than is to be found at Quebec or Montreal."
"There is but one course open for securing that
quota of the western trade which the advantages of
the St. Lawrence route give us reason to anticipate.
If we can give to the owners of the largest vessels
now profitably engaged in the trade of Lake Michigan
the option of trading to Kingston and the St. Lawrence, or to Buffalo, as may be found most profitable,
we shall have thrown down the barrier which now
forces the main current of trade into the Erie canal.
We shall have more than balanced the greater insur-

ance and freights charged from our seaports to
Europe over the corresponding charges from New
York, and we may thereafter expect Quebec and
Montreal to take rank among the greatest grain
marts of this continent.''

The value of the navigation of the Canadian
canals can, I think, be safely inferred from this
report of the Canadian minister of finance. Notwithstanding the importance attached to it by the
inhabitants of the northwest, the results of its practical use for a series of years were unsatisfactory if
not insignificant. In spite of every effort to direct
the carrying trade from the Erie canal the Canadian
canals obtained only a small fraction of the total
trade, and this small fraction seemed to bear a
smaller and smaller proportion to the total traffic
between the west and the sea-coast.

An examination of the history and effect of the
reciprocity treaty of 1854 leads to the conclusion that
the measure was favorable to the development of
trade between the United States and the British
provinces. The statistics of trade indicate a greater
increase of commerce during the continuance of the
treaty than at any other time during the period from
1820 1880. This increase appears most clearly
during the early years of the treaty, for the later
years were disturbed by extraordinary economic
events. But dependence must not be had exclusively
upon statistics, for there were features of the trade
which cannot be illustrated by means of statistics.
The ''commerce of convenience'' and the gain to
both countries, and especially to the United States,
of obtaining raw materials free of duty are subjects
incapable of statistical illustration. Imperfections

there may have been, and certainly were, as was
most natural in a first attempt at the settlement of
trade relations on a new basis.   These imperfections,
however, were not the cause of its abrogation.   The
cause was political rather than economical or commercial.   There is very little doubt, as has been said
already, that the attitude of the English towards the
North during the civil war, was the direct cause of
the abrogation of the treaty.   The evident hostility
of the English aroused still more fully all the dormant
resentment of the North, stirred as it was already
by the southern rebellion.   In such a state of feeling
the result of any discussion of the treaty must prove
fatal.   And so it did.   The controversy in regard to
renewal began just as the hostility to England was
strongest.   The arguments of the friends of reciprocity were of no avail.   The opponents of the
measure appealed to the patriotism of the people,
and to their self-interest as well.   They showed the
great loss of revenue caused by the existence of the
treaty; they made it clear that the British colonists
were profiting from the needs of the Americans; and
they clinched the argument by reminding the people
of the hostility of those very people who were grow-
ing rich from their necessities.   The majority are
moved more by their feelings than by their judg-
ment.   The business sentiment of the country
favored a continuance of the policy of reciprocity,
but it was overruled by the burst of patriotic feeling
aroused throughout the nation.

The unfortunate fate of the reciprocity treaty has
given it a false position in the economic history of
the country.   As the first measure of its kind in the
trade relations of the United States and Canada and

with no successor as yet, it seems an isolated thing, unrelated to the preceding or succeeding periods. But this was not really the case. The years from 1846–1870 witnessed the development of a policy on the part of the principal nations of the world in favor of the removal of many of the existing restrictions upon international trade. This policy was shown by the repeal of the corn laws in England, by the develpment of the zollverein in Germany, by the negotiation of numerous commercial treaties and by the reduction of import duties in various countries. In the United States the tendency found expression in the negotiation of the reciprocity treaty and in the reduced tariffs of 1846 and 1857. But this movement, unfortunately, was interrupted by the outbreak of the civil war in the United States and by the Franco-Prussian war in Europe. The consequence of these two events was the overthrow of the liberal movement in Europe and America. The United States needed greater revenues for the conduct of the war and for the payment of the debt thus incurred. Europe since 1870 has been an armed camp, and enormous revenues are needed to keep in constant readiness the millions of soldiers, the large navies and the costly defences required in such a state of affairs. With the downfall of the liberal movement disappeared the best hopes of better trade relations between the United States and the British provinces.

APPENDIX.

1820–1850.

TRADE BETWEEN THE UNITED STATES AND THE BRITISH PROVINCES.

Year.	Imports United States from British North America.	Exports United States to British North America.
1821	$490,704	$2,009,791
1822	526,817	1,897,559
1823	463,374	1,821,460
1824	705,931	1,775,724
1825	610,788	2,539,964
1826	650,316	2,588,549
1827	445,118	2,830,674
1828	447,659	1,674,674
1829	577,542	2,764,909
1830	650,303	3,786,373
1831	864,909	4,061,838
1832	1,229,526	3,614,385
1833	1,793,393	4,471,084
1834	1,548,733	3,535,276
1835	1,435,168	4,047,888
1836	2,427,571	2,651,266
1837	2,359,263	3,288,966
1838	1,555,570	2,723,491
1839	2,155,146	3,563,454
1840	2,007,767	6,100,001
1841	1,968,187	6,656,563
1842	1,762,001	6,190,309
1843	857,696	2,724,422
1844	1,465,715	6,715,903
1845	2,020,065	6,054,226
1846	1,937,717	7,406,433
1847	2,343,937	7,985,543
1848	3,646,467	8,382,655
1849	2,826,880	8,104,267

The preceding table is taken from the report of the committee on commerce of the House of Representatives, which was drawn up by Elijah Ward and was presented in April, 1864. It is in the "Reports of Committees," First Session, Thirty-eighth Congress, 1863-1864, Vol. I, No. 39, p. 1-2.

1850-1885.

TRADE BETWEEN THE UNITED STATES AND THE BRITISH PROVINCES.

Year.	Imports United States from British North America.	British North America from United States.
1850	5,179,500	11,608,641
1851	5,279,718	14,263,751
1852	5,469,445	13,993,570
1853	6,527,559	19,445,478
1854	8,784,412	26,115,132
1855	15,118,289	34,862,188
1856	21,276,614	35,764,980
1857	22,108,916	27,788,238
1858	15,784,836	22,210,837
1859	19,287,565	26,761,618
1860	23,572,796	25,871,399
1861	22,724,489	28,520,735
1862	18,515,685	30,373,212
1863	17,191,217	29,680,955
1864	29,608,736	7,952,401
1865	33,264,403	27,269,158
1866	48,528,628	27,905,984
1867	25,044,005	25,239,459
1868	26,261,378	22,644,235
1869	29,293,766	21,680,062
1870	36,265,328	21,869,447
1871	32,542,137	27,185,586
1872	36,346,930	33,741,995
1873	37,175,244	45,193,042
1874	34,173,586	51,785,154
1875	27,866,615	48,641,477
1876	28,805,964	43,873,789
1877	24,164,755	51,568,164

Year.	Imports United States from British North America	British North America from United States.
1878	25,044,811	49,186,384
1879	25,719,771	43,957.284
1880	32,988,564	40,610,949
1881	37,684,101	49,346,371
1882	50,775,581	53,201,161
1883	44,294,158	62,855,790
1884	38,399,835	57,740,714
1885	36,695,685	51,518,335

These figures are from the " Quarterly Reports of the Bureau of Statistics," 1885–1886, p. 371. The data for the United States are for fiscal year ending June 30. Those for the British provinces, 1850–1863, are for the calendar year. Those for 1864 for the British provinces are for six months ending June 30, 1864.

EXPORTS TO CANADA AND THE PROVINCES.

Year.	Domestic.	Foreign.
1821	2,009,336	455.
1822	1,881,273	16,286
1823	1,818,113	3,347
1824	1,773,107	2,617
1825	2,538,224	1,740
1826	2,564,165	24,384
1827	2,797,014	33,660
1828	1,618,288	56,386
1829	3,724,104	40,805
1830	3,650,031	136,342
1831	4,026,392	35,416
1832	3,569,302	45,083
1833	4,390,081	81,003
1834	3,477,709	57,567
1835	3,900,545	14,343
1836	2,456,415	194,851
1837	2,992,474	296,512
1838	2,484,987	238,504
1839	3,418,770	144,684
1840	5,895,966	204,035

Year.	Domestic.	Foreign.
1841..........	6,292,290	364,273
1842..........	5,950,143	240,166
1843..........	2,617,005	107,417
1844·······....	5,361,186	1,354,717
1845..........	4,844,966	1,209,260
1846..........	6,042,666	1,363,767
1847..........	5,819,667	2,165,876
1848..........	6,399,959	1,982,696
1849..........	5,932,106	2,172,161
1850..........	7,758,291	1,790,744
1851..........	9,060,387	2,954,536
1852..........	6,655,097	3,853,919
1853..........	7,404,087	5,736,555
1854..........	15,204,144	9,362,716
1855..........	15,806,642	11,999,378
1856..........	22,714,697	6,314,652
1857..........	19,936,113	4,326,369
1858..........	19,338,959	4,012,768
1859..........	18,029,254	6,622,473
1860..........	18,667,429	4,038,899
1861..........	18,883,715	3,861,098
1862..........	18,652,012	2,427,103
1863..........	28,629,110	2,651,920

"House Executive Documents," 1863-1864, Vol. 9, No. 32, p. 6.
Years end September 30, 1821-1842, and June 30, 1843-1863.

STATEMENT EXHIBITING IN CONTRAST THE VALUE OF EACH CLASS OF
IMPORTS, INTO THE UNITED STATES AND THE PROVINCE
OF CANADA, FROM THE OTHER, UNDER
THE TREATY.

	1850.		1851.		1852.	
	Into U. S.	Into Canada.	Into U. S.	Into Canada.	Into U. S.	Into Canada.
Products of the Mine.	——---	41,587	17,623	62,516	192	64,857
Products of the Forest	1,539,488	45,505	1,279,929	18,620	1,838,775	116,159
Products of the Sea...	30,943	21,473	43,784	26,494	50,289	31,079
Animals and Products	490,477	455,036	564,787	962,176	966,189	454,475
Agricultural Products	2,706,362	427,084	1,937.293	676,327	3,277,929	473,137
Total..............	4,767,270	990,685	3,843,416	1,746,133	6,133,374	1,139,707

	1853.		1854.		1855.	
	Into U. S.	Into Canada.	Into U. S.	Into Canada.	It to U. S.	Into Canada.
Products of the Mine.	58,400	126,586	118,628	256,182	23,303	425,739
Products of the Forest	2,589,898	66,620	2,131,725	107,459	3,016,880	186,830
Products of the Sea..	73,422	383,436	85,472	74,851	148,550	261,853
Animals and Products	1,107,870	570,587	684,439	845,591	1,485,925	1,878,664
Agricultural Products	4,949,576	668,113	5,295,667	1,500,521	11,801,435	4,972.475
Total..............	8,779,166	1,815,342	8.305,931	2,784,604	16,476,' 93	7,725,561

	1856.		1857.		1858.	
	Into U. S.	Into Canada.	Into U. S.	Into Canada.	Into U. S.	Into Canada.
Products of the Mine.	84,228	488,984	189,894	509,494	93,405	324,374
Products of the Forest	3,345,284	3 2,904	3,393,068	411,820	3,200,383	232,177
Products of the Sea ..	140,948	411,716	154,417	314,228	168,485	157,674
Animals and Products	2,375,388	2,896,838	1,974,516	2,134,339	2,231,786	1,464,873
Agricultural Products	11,864,636	3,809,112	7,100,413	5,272,151	5,749,305	3,385,517
Total	17,810,684	7,909,554	12,812,308	8,642,030	11,514,364	5,564,615

	1859.		1860.		1862.		1863.	
	Into U. S.	Into Canada.	Into U. S.	Into Canada.	Into U. S.	Into Canada.	Into U. S.	Into Canada.
Products of the Mine.	227,911	328,139	318,537	406,688	1,073,565	510,081	1,114,831	647,905
Products of the Forest	3,524,850	162,113	4,010,278	137,392	2,980,477	181,519	3,679,559	134,281
Products of the Sea...	201,583	183,575	185,873	227,112	1,087,013	268,045	957,166	281,023
Animals and Products	3,391,772	1,758,428	3,557,912	1,679,912	3,124,203	2,658,217	3,133.463	3,050,294
Agricultural Products	6,278,351	4,671,882	10,013,799	4,603,114	8,860,002	17,717,846	7,005,826	8,137,447
Total	13,624,467	7,104,137	18,095,399	7,054,218	17,116,260	14,335 708	15,890,845	12,251,010

The statistics for the years 1850-1860 are from the Reports of Committees (House), Vol. 3, No. 22, p. 36.

Those for 1862-1863 are my own, calculated from the returns of the Minister of Finance of Canada and the Secretary of the Treasury of the United States given in their reports, p. 40, note.

IMPORTS INTO CANADA FROM UNITED STATES.

	Value of Free Goods.	Dutiable Goods.	Total Imports.	Amount Duties Paid.	Rate.
1850....	791,128	5,803,732	6,594,860	1,069,814	18.43
1851 ...	1,384,030	6,981,735	8,365,765	1,274,702	18.26
1852....	864,690	7,613,003	8,477,693	1,433,195	18.82
1853....	1,125,565	10,656,582	11,782,147	1,805,812	16.94
1854....	2,083,757	13,449,341	15,533,098	2,209,173	16.42
1855....	9,379,204	11,449,472	20,828,676	1,786,032	15.60
1856...	9,933,586	12,770,923	22,704,509	2,059,826	16.13
1857....	10,258,221	9,966,430	20,224,651	1,605,164	16.10
1858 ...	7,161,958	8,473,607	15,635,565	1,611,711	19.02
1859....	8,560,055	9,032,861	17,592,916	1,825,135	20.20
1860....	8,746,799	8,526,230	17,273,029	1,759,928	20.64
1861...	12,730,768	8,338,620	25,069,388	1,584,892	19.00
1862....	19,044,374	6,128,783	25,173,157		

"House Executive Document," 1863–64, Vol. 9, No. 32, p. 8. Calendar year.

"Report of A. T. Galt, Minister of Finance," March, 1862, p. 19, except for 1862.

TOTAL IMPORT FROM CANADA AND PROVINCES.

	Free by Ordinary Laws.	Free by Treaty.	Total Free.	Paying Duty.	Total Imports.
1850....................	787,599		787,599	4,856,863	5,344,462
1851....................	1,690,052		1,690,052	5,003,070	6,093,122
1852....................	980,289		980,289	5,130,010	6,110,299
1853....................	1,418,250		1,418,250	6,132,468	7,550,718
1854....................	639,143		639,143	8,288,417	8,927,560
1855....................	906,786	7,197,337	8,104,123	7,032,611	15,136,734
1856....................	1,081,611	19,407,086	20,488,697	821,724	21,310,421
1857....................	1,016,342	20,280,210	21,296,552	827,744	22,124,296
1858....................	562,532	14,752,255	15,314,787	491,732	15,806,519
1859....................	2,609,420	16,384,416	18,983,836	733,715	19,727,551
1860....................	2,734,385	20,446,586	23,180,971	690,411	23,851,381
1861....................	2,494,997	20,047,525	22,542,522	520,411	23,062,833
1862....................	1,618,185	17,152,552	18,770,737	529,258	19,299,995
1863....................		15,780,343		872,282	

"House Executive Documents," 1863–64; Vol. 9, No. 32, p. 7; year ending June 30.

EXPORTS FROM UNITED STATES TO CANADA AND OTHER PROVINCES.

Year.	Exports United States to Canada.	United States to Other Provinces.
1849	4,234,724	3,869,543
1850	5,930,821	3,618,214
1851	7,929,140	4,085,783
1852	6,717,060	3,791,956
1853	7,829,099	5,311,543
1854	17,300,706	7,266,154
1855	18,720,344	9,085,676
1856	20,883,241	8,146,108
1757	16,574,895	7,637,587
1858	17,029,254	6,622,473
1859	18,940,792	9,213,832
1860	14,083,114	8,623,214
1861	14,361,858	8,383,755
1862	12,842,504	8,236,611
1863	19,898,718	11,382,312

From "House Executive Documents," first session Thirty-eighth Congress, 1863-1864, Vol. IX, No. 32, p. 5.   The years end June 30.

Year.	Imports United States from Canada.	United States from Other Provinces.
1850	4,285,470	1,358,992
1851	4,956,471	1,736,651
1852	4,589,969	1,520,330
1853	5,278,116	2,272,602
1854	6,721,539	2,206,021
1855	12,182,314	2,954,420
1856	17,488,197	3,822,224
1857	18,291,834	3,832,462
1858	11,581,571	4,224,948
1859	14,208,717	5,518,834
1860	18,861,673	4,989,708
1861	18,645,457	4,417,476
1862	15,253,152	4,046,843
1863	18,816,999	

From "House Executive Documents," first session Thirty-eighth Congress, 1863-1864; Vol. IX, No 32, pp. 6-7.   The years are fiscal years, ending June 30.

LEADING EXPORTS TO BRITISH PROVINCES OTHER THAN CANADA, FROM 1849-1863.

	Wheat.	Wheat Flour.	Indian Corn.	Meal, Corn and Rye.
June 30, 1849........	332,765	1.518,922	126,791	625,691
1850........	214,779	1,051,546	57,731	421,112
1851........	220,319	945,397	66,169	289,510
1852........	165,106	688,956	86,221	137,718
1853........	208,956	784,498	105 404	135,040
1854........	216,266	955,484	149,688	378,295
1855........	182,614	1,753,395	154 214	702,204
1856..... ..	268,959	3,120,787	130,774	631,059
1857........	221,560	2,881 803	98,340	370,774
1858........	132,187	2 618,913	85,210	248,420
1859........	100,717	2,982,171	93,320	209,049
1860........	90,049	3,044,243	85,915	208,881
1861........	26,563	3,065.210	40,875	108,029
1862........	16,582	3,190,208	65,358	254,182
1863........	110,333	4,420,748	131,552	280,238

"House Executive Documents," 1863–1864, Vol. IX, No. 32, p. 18.

1858-1863.

MANUFACTURES EXPORTED BY UNITED STATES TO PROVINCE OF CANADA.

	1858-59.	1859-60.	1860-61.	1861-62.	1862-63.
Cotton Manufactures..........	$363,016	314,491	403,591	246,442	64,495
Hemp " { including Cordage,	32,702	21,971	43,664	16,378	10,565
Iron Manufactures { except Pig Iron,	761,619	716,507	839,421	773,381	395,907
Leather, Boots and Shoes......	211,147	137,475	106,648	68,770	22,860
Tobacco manufactured........	1,205,684	863,934	683,875	203,681	78,026
Glassware.	85,232	77,061	83,950	121,381	87,032
Earthenware	9,350	11,151	12,347	12,147	8,244
House Furniture..............	136,765	123,251	124,250	188,820	66,718
India-rubber Manufactures...	13,217	5,036	10,158	1,151	528
Carriages.....................	20,449	109,419	11,117	35,054	11,501
Books	154,034	70,134	106,524	62,838	25,164
Paper and Stationery..........	78,825	61,433	74,272	72,378	55,171
Jewelry....	15,960	5,760	12,954	11,046	5,044
Hats................	116,150	90,100	79,016	49,505	14,078
Tin Manufactures............	15,451	20,565	4,362	1,375	
Marble & Stone Manufactures.	53,883	100,009	97,977	97,002	48,293
Trunks and Umbrellas........	5,470	1,575,	2,577	1,367	1,434
Clothing....................	9,373	16,655	11,163	8,404	1,328
Wood Manufactures..........	45,146	43,547	36,593	49,061	58,302
Candles and Soap.............	11,450	8,079	9,558	4,583	2,428
Paints and Varnish..........	27,163	32 521	39,903	39,646	30,094
Copper & Brass Manufactures .	60,511	49,658	16,909	32,238	50,874
Musical Instruments..........	104,534	91,732	122,800	100,007	67,445
Printing Materials...........	1,771	3,437	5,544	4,259	1,280
Other Enumerated............	21,990	5,595	12,776	8,190	4,784
Unenumerated	624,534	542,028	549,903	388,220	401,227
Total...........	4,185,516	3,548,114	3,501,642	2,596,930	1,510,802

This table is from report of April, 1864, "House Reports," First Session, Thirty-eighth Congress, Vol. I. 39, p. 5.

See also "House Executive Documents," First Session, Thirty-eighth Congress, 1863–1864, Vol. IX. No. 32, p. 15.

•

ENTERED.

Nationality of vessels employed in the carrying trade between the United States and British North American provinces :

Year.	American.	Foreign Tonnags.
1857–58 from Canada..............	1,240,159	1,105,356
From other B. N. A. provinces....	138,640	382,712
1858–59 from Canada..............	1,344,717	922,920
From other B. N. A. provinces....	171,024	390,926
1859-60 from Canada..............	1,936,955	957,063
From other B. N. A. provinces....	229,749	411,432
1860-61 from Canada..............	2,617,276	658,036
From other B. N. A. provinces....	184,062	475,051
1861–62 from Canada..............	1,996,892	684,879
From other B. N. A. provinces....	196,709	465,141
Total..........................10,056,183		6,453,520

CLEARED.

Nationality of vessels employed in the carrying trade between the United States and British North American provinces :

Year.	American.	Foreign Tonnage.
1857–58 to Canada.................	1,133,584	1,104,650
To other B. N. A. provinces.......	319,985	461,245
1858–59 to Canada.................	1,364,580	1,012,358
To other B. N. A. provinces.......	242,407	475,329
1859-60 to Canada.................	1,982,586	1,083,566
To other B. N. A. provinces.......	371,257	516,646
1860-61 to Canada.................	2,678,276	896,124
To other B. N. A. provinces.......	291,812	599,430
1861-62 to Canada.................	2,025,670	731,123
To other B. N. A. provinces.......	297,172	509,928
Total..........................10,707,329		7,391,399

"Reports of Committee." (House) 1863–64, Vol. I, No. 39, p. 6.

Value of goods passing through the United States to Canada under bond :

1855	4,463,774
1856	4,926,922
1857	5,582,643
1858	2,057,024
1859	4,546,491
1860	3,041,877
1861	5,688,952
1862	5,508,427
1863	

"House Executive Documents." 1863–1864, Vol. IX, No. 32, p. 36, from Canadian records. The principal portion of this trade passes over the railroad line, entering Canada at Island Pond, Vermont (by the Grand Trunk).

PRINCIPAL REFERENCES.

"House Executive Documents," 1849-1850; Vol. 8, No. 64.
"Message of President Taylor upon Reciprocal Trade with
Canada," with correspondence, May, 1850.

"House Executive Documents," 1851-1852; Vol. 2, part 1, No. 2,
pp. 83-92. "Annual Message" of President Fillmore, December,
1851; with correspondence upon commercial intercourse with
Canada.

"House Executive Documents," 1852-1853; Vol. 4, No. 40. "Message" of President Fillmore transmitting "Report of the Secretary
of State upon the Negotiations for Reciprocity with Canada."

"Reports of Committees," (House) 1852-53, No. 4. "Report of
Committee on Commerce on Reciprocal Trade with the British
North American Colonies;" with statistics and correspondence.

The *Congressional Globe*; especially Part 3, 1863-1864, May 18, 19,
24, 25 and 26, 1864; containing the principal debate in the House
upon the treaty; and Part 1, 1864-1865, January 11 and 12, 1865,
containing the principal debate in the Senate.

"House Executive Documents," 1859-1860, Vol. 13, No. 96.
Report of Israel T. Hatch and James W. Taylor upon the treaty.

"Reports of Committees" (House) 1861-1862; Vol. 3, No. 22.
Report of Committee on Commerce upon the treaty, prepared by
Elijah Ward, of New York.

"Report of the Minister of Finance, A. T. Galt, of Canada, upon
the 'Report of the Committee on Commerce of the House of Representatives of the United States.' A reply to the preceding
Report." March, 1862.

"House Executive Documents," 1863-64; Vol. 9, No. 32. Letter
from Secretary of Treasury on treaty, with many statistical tables.

"Reports of Committees" (House) 1863-64; Vol. 1, No. 39.
Report of committee on commerce upon the treaty, prepared
by Elijah Ward of New York.

"Proceedings of the Commercial Convention held in Detroit
July 11-14, 1865." Published by order of the convention. Detroit,
1865.

"Speeches on Commercial, financial and other subjects of Elijah Ward," New York, 1877; especially pp. 59–87 and 88–99. Speeches delivered in the House of Representatives May 18 and 26, 1864.

"Canada and the States. Recollections, 1851–1885. Sir E. W. Watkin," London, 1887. Chap. XVIII, pp. 374–430. "The Reciprocity Treaty with the United States."

"Life of Lawrence Oliphant." Mrs. M. O. W. Oliphant, New York, 1891, two volumes. Vol. I, Chap IV, 106–132.

"Episodes in a Life of Adventure." Lawrence Oliphant, New York, 1887, Chap. III, 32–48.

·

PUBLICATIONS

OF THE

AMERICAN

ECONOMIC ASSOCIATION

VOLUME VII

AMERICAN ECONOMIC ASSOCIATION,

1892.

CONTENTS OF VOLUME VII.

AMERICAN ECONOMIC ASSOCIATION.

Organized at Saratoga, September 9th, 1885.

OFFICERS.

President:
FRANCIS A. WALKER, LL. D.

Vice-Presidents:
CHARLES F. DUNBAR, A. B.
WILLIAM W. FOLWELL, LL. D.
CARROLL D. WRIGHT, A. M.

Secretary:
RICHARD T. ELY, Ph. D.,
University of Wisconsin, Madison, Wis.

Treasurer:
FREDERICK B. HAWLEY, A. M.,
141 Pearl Street, New York City.

PUBLICATION COMMITTEE.

F. H. GIDDINGS, A. M., *Chairman.*
Bryn Mawr College, Bryn Mawr, Pa.
H. C. ADAMS, Ph. D.
J. B. CLARK, Ph. D.
E. R. A. SELIGMAN, Ph. D.
F. W. TAUSSIG, Ph. D.

Resolution of the Council.—All monographs or other scientific publications shall bear the names of the Committee on Publication.

All communications of an editorial nature should be addressed to Prof. F. H. GIDDINGS, Bryn Mawr, Pa.
Orders for monographs and all communications of a business nature should be addressed to the PUBLICATION AGENT, AMERICAN ECONOMIC ASSOCIATION, Baltimore, Md.

EXTRACT FROM THE CONSTITUTION.

ARTICLE IV.—MEMBERSHIP.

Any person may become a member of this Association by paying three dollars, and after the first year may continue a member by paying an annual fee of three dollars. On payment of fifty dollars any person may become a life-member, exempt from annual dues.

Note.—Each member shall be entitled to receive all reports and publications of the Association.

ERRATA.

Nos. 2 and 3

On the Shifting and Incidence of Taxation.

Page 18, Line 1. Erase part.

" 27, " 15. For France read France".

." 47, Note 1, Line 12. For "Cort read Cort.

" 47, " 1, " 12. " Leerboek read "Leerboek.

" 47, " 2, " 2. " Wages Question read "The Wages Question".

" 55, " 1, " 3. " L'Impôt read "L'Impôt".

" 71, " 1, " 1. " Grundsäte read Grundsätze.

" 71, " 2, " 1. " Ruckwälzung read Rückwälzung.

" 72, Note 2 should follow Note 1.

" 90, Line 12. For area greed read are agreed,

" 98, Note 1, Line 2. For 16 read 164.

" 100, " 1, " 2. " "In his Reports read In his "Reports.

" 109, Note. For 62 read 60.

" 122, Note, Line 7. For 132 read 126.

" 127, Note 1, Line 1. For 127 read 121.

" 135, " , " 2. " "his Einleitung read his "Einleitung.

" 149, Line 18. Erase by.

" 156, Note, Line 15. For EO, read FO.

" 166, Note 1, Line 1. For 101 read 95.

" 167, Note, Line 1. For 137 read 130.

" 183, Note. For 91 read 89.

" 189, 3 lines from bottom For Maquis read Marquis.

" 190, Line 14, For fur read für.

" 190. For Stewart, James read Steuart, James.

" 190. " Steuart, Dugald read Stewart, Dugald.

INDEX.

VOLUME VII.

Publications of the American Economic Association.

www.ingramcontent.com/pod-product-compliance
Lightning Source LLC
Chambersburg PA
CBHW031455270326
41930CB00007B/1014